New York City Travel Guide

The Most Up-To-Date Pocket Guide To Discovering New York's Hidden Treasures, the Most Beautiful Skyscrapers Sights, and Experience an Unforgettable Vacation

Tad Parker

Table of Contents

Introduction

New York City is unrivaled in terms of its vibrancy, cultural significance, and sheer diversity. It's all here, in plenty and at its best: high finance, fine art, architecture, music, and cuisine. You can sample different cuisines from around the world whether you're eating or drinking, dressing up in quick or couture fashion, gawking at subversive street art or ancient master paintings at the Met, or stumbling across a Midtown movie set. The Statue of Liberty with her torch lifted, the flashing lights of Times Square, the majestic Empire State Building, or the waterfront promenade in Brooklyn Heights are just a few examples of the popular culture icons that are frequently right in front of you.

Having said that, the city expects more than simply a scuff on a well-worn surface. Dig deeper - stay a week or two; move past Central Park and the famous museums on the Upper East and

West sides, past the historical highlights of downtown and Midtown, and on to lesser-known neighborhoods, buildings, green spaces and art collections; let yourself be diverted by a tree-lined street or stray path, a glimpse of an Art Deco detail, a hole-in-the-wall serving soul food or fried dumplings - and you'll start to feel a new rhythm. New York certainly has a lot of excitement, but it also has a subtle charm. Discover it in secret gardens next to postmodern skyscrap22ers, priceless artwork hidden away in modest lobbies, the mansions of robber barons, and fake medieval cloisters, a riverside where you can bike, kayak, or just stroll along to take in the view, or the late-night vibe in a Harlem jazz joint, underground Brooklyn rock club, or even around a street-food cart in Jackson Heights, Queens. Exploring is one of the city's greatest joys, and each borough has its own attractions, so having a feeling of adventure is essential to the experience. You are welcome to spend time at each attraction, but if you want to see the dazzling metropolis from the Staten Island Ferry, enjoy a great espresso in a shabby-chic Williamsburg café, or celebrate by getting a taco after taking the "A" to the Rockaways, get moving.

Chapter 1:

Things to Know Before You Go

At first appearance, New York can appear to be a pretty intimidating place. The sheer size and infinite activity of this metropolis, which has over 8.5 million residents and nearly as many tourists (during the busy season), might fatigue you as soon as you arrive. But have courage. In essence, New York is little more than a collection of small towns, each with its own distinct character and a range of activities and attractions. Being the bold, daring lady that you are, your goal is to discover as many of them as you can.

And we're ready to assist!

Knowing insider information about a vacation spot is half the battle won if you've ever returned from a trip wishing you had known it beforehand. Here are our most insightful insider advice on everything you should know...before you leave, in order to achieve this and to aid you in properly planning your vacation.

The finest seasons to visit New York are Fall (Sept to Nov) and Spring (March to June), with the former being preferred to the occasionally too-wet latter. If you have the opportunity of choosing your travel dates, try to avoid the blisteringly cold and oppressively hot months of winter and summer in New York. Check the Holiday Weather Website for annual and monthly averages, but keep in mind that the humidity in the summer and the high wind factor in the winter might cause temperatures to seem quite a few degrees off the expected norm.

Where to stay: Unlike many other cities across the world, choosing a specific borough to stay in (New York has five) is "nearly" unimportant because attractions are dispersed throughout all five, each has its own charm and joys, and getting around on the subway and by foot is incredibly simple. Everyone's dream vacation includes lodging in Manhattan's Central Park neighborhood, but this is also the most expensive option you could find. In any location, staying in a budget hotel, hostel, or B&B is your best option. Spending all of your hard-earned vacation money on lodging for a room you'll probably just use for sleep is not the best use of your time in New York. For more information, see our thorough guide to New York.

Prepare to stroll. All over - Everyone in New York fits the stereotype of an amateur athlete, and they all have toned calf muscles to prove it. Because they walk everywhere, this is. Although we'll guide you through the city's metro system, be aware that whether you like it or not, you'll be walking an excessive lot in this city. Cabs may be common and reasonably priced, but because to the city's unpredictable traffic, they can also be laughably inefficient unless you want to spend the most of your time stopped at traffic lights.

After only one day, you'll understand how invaluable comfortable walking shoes and thick socks are in New York City. Pack both of these items. It's true that Manolo Blanks are far sexier than Nikes, but it's not attractive to walk around the city like a zombie with hurting legs. Keep your heels at home as a favor to yourself.

Spend $20 on impromptu foot massages in Chinatown; they're almost as valuable as a pair of comfortable, flat-soled shoes.

Therefore, don't worry about dressing up because New Yorkers are among the world's trendiest dressers all the time. But the truth is that they enjoy dressing casually just as much as the next weary traveller, so don't worry about seeming unprepared. especially in Broadway theaters! Although a select few customers dress to the nines, the most arrive in jeans and sneakers. Most likely because it took them 12 blocks to get to the theater!

Do not be afraid of the subway - The New York subway can initially look intimidating, but if you get the feel of it, it's pretty simple. Additionally, New Yorkers are very hospitable (particularly to international tourists), so don't be afraid to ask the locals for assistance or directions. You'll be ready to travel if you have a great subway app on your pocket.

Friendly but impatient, New Yorkers The people of New York are generally incredibly nice, unless you suddenly stop in the middle of a sidewalk or subway exit. They can then explode in rage. The speed of life around here is really rapid—possibly faster than in any other major city. Locals move about as quickly as they talk and drive, and footpaths resemble motorways. You won't hear the end of it if you get in their way.

Carry a bottle of water. This will help you save money and plastic because it's simple to refill in cafes, restaurants, and even museums.

While New York City may have a few public restrooms here and there, Murphy's Law states that you'll never locate one when you need one. Instead, treat restrooms like the hidden gems they are. Additionally, the town's public restrooms are not the cleanest. Use one whenever you see one, especially in fast-food restaurants like Starbucks and McDonald's, as well as in public libraries and museums.

Even if you travel during the height of summer, you might not understand how breezy a city like New York can be. Dress in layers and be prepared for cool temperatures. Due to the dense concentration of high-rise buildings in the CBD, street temperatures—many of which receive no sunlight at all—can easily be 10 degrees lower than the daily average. In addition, air conditioning is highly valued at this region, so you'll always find it cold in theaters, museums, and movie theaters, as well as at the top of the Empire State Building. Follow local custom and place a small travel umbrella and a sweater or cardigan in your handbag each day.

Don't forget Top of the Rock - The Rockefeller Centre's rooftop observatory is the best place to see the city, even surpassing the more well-known Empire State Building. The views are greater, everything goes much more smoothly, and, let's face it, the Empire State Building is a beautiful landmark to see from rather than from. A visit here at sunset is unmatched!

Beware of tourist traps: Despite being veritable tourist traps, two of the city's most notable landmarks are still worthwhile to visit for various reasons. The 9-11 Memorial Museum is extremely moving, but it draws the kind of throng that would drive even the most holistic guru insane. You might easily lose two hours just waiting in line for tickets if you don't reserve your space online BEFORE you come. Be aware that the New York City Pass just recently included this attraction. The chapter titled "Get in & Get Around" has further information about this pass. Times Square is the second big trap in this area, and despite how great it is, it should be avoided after the first visit. You ought to watch it at least once. Sure? Is this the best place for you to shop, eat, and drink? No! Feel free to go there, snap a selfie, and then leave because everything is pricey, overcrowded, and commercialized.

Spot a famous person? Play it cool - It could be difficult to maintain your composure if you see your favorite star out and about on Fifth Avenue, but that's exactly what you need to do. The city is renowned for providing anonymity to the wealthy and famous, and New Yorkers value this philosophy beyond all else. So feel free to be all mushy inside, but remember that approaching a famous person and asking for a picture or autograph is seen as quite uncool.

Don't miss the Highline—this stunning elevated urban park is a totally original idea. Take advantage of the opportunity to promenade above the city even though New York is home to THE urban park.

Know when museums are free to enter - Would you rather spend money on shoes than on museums? Easy as pie! While many of the city's museums are open to the public at all times, some of the larger ones additionally provide special days or hours during which admission is free. A little donation is occasionally welcomed but never required. This is an excellent alternative if you want to visit a few museums but don't want to spend money on a tourist ticket. You should be able to witness at least two of the "free times" because the majority occur on Fridays, even though you won't be able to attend all of them. Visit the NYC Arts Website for a detailed list of everything that is free.

and all other unrestricted pursuits – The mere notion of how "expensive" their city is makes New Yorkers scoff, and the majority of them frequently respond that this is, in fact, a ridiculous exaggeration. However, there is constantly a ton of free items available. They will yell and protest, and the majority of the time, they are right. No matter what time of year you visit, there is always plenty of exciting free stuff to see and do thanks to the city's busy schedule.

But be careful not to overschedule your day. Some people contend that "free time" should be the one item on your New York schedule that you absolutely must include. Time free from touring, admiring landmarks, taking photos, or going to shows. Time in New York to simply be, with no plans whatsoever. It's time to go lost, find yourself, and explore the 1001 incredible little-known secrets that make this city so alluring. Therefore, fill it up and leave exactly as much out. and your trip to New York City will undoubtedly be much more pleasurable and less stressful.

Chapter 2:
Arriving in New York City

Once in New York, you can get to Manhattan by taxi, shuttle, public transportation, or NYC Limos. There isn't a single best or least expensive option that applies to everyone because it depends on your spending limit, the volume of your luggage, your availability, the number of people in your group, and the time of day. A (very pleased) buddy of mine once told me,

Taxis in New York City

Taxis (yellow cabs) often have a metered fare based on the trip's distance and duration. The fixed amount they charge to and from JFK airport is an exception. Metered fees are applied at both LGA and EWR airports. In any cab ride, all tolls and tips are your responsibility. The following are the general prices, including tips and tolls, for each direction:

LGA - $40 meter charge each way, maximum of 4 passengers.

JFK: set rate of $70 roundtrip for up to 4 passengers.

EWR -$95 metered rate inbound, additional charges outbound, up to 4 people

The majority of taxis can accommodate up to four passengers, although airports occasionally have taxi vans that can accommodate six passengers for the same price as standard taxis. When purchasing your flights, keep in mind the additional expenses related to EWR that were previously outlined.

Limos in New York City

The prices and services offered by NYC Limos, sometimes known as "black cars" or "town cars," are essentially same. You can hire a NYC limo of your choosing based on the number of people in your group. Their prices frequently match those of taxi cabs and, in some cases, are considerably less because to internet discounts and offers. As you depart the airport, there will almost always be "limo" drivers attempting to offer you an on-the-spot, unreserved ride. These are known as "gypsy cabs," are prohibited. Rely on a licensed yellow cab or a hired limo from a trustworthy provider. In NYC, Uber is still relatively new and may or may not work.

They frequently charge substantially more than taxis do. But UberPOOL is a fantastic addition to NYC.

The large NYC limo firms have the advantage of keeping their vehicles in parking lots within five minutes from each of the three main airports. If you hire a car ahead of time and your flight is delayed, you can be charged extra for the wait period. Prepare to go back to the parking lot with the driver since reserved cars must also park and wait for you near baggage claim with a sign. Upon arrival at baggage claim, you may use any pay phone to contact NYC Limos at no cost. This may be the quickest and least expensive option to rent a NYC limo when traveling with fewer than five individuals.

Carmel and Skyline are two companies that come highly recommended.

Carmel Limo: 866-666-6666, www.carmellimo.com

Skyline Car Service: 800-533-6325, www.skylineride.com

For coupons and discounts, see

NYC Limos (link:https://www.nycinsiderguide.com/nyc-limos). In general, Limos from the airport are not the same companies to be used for a private limousine tour of NYC.

Airport Shuttles

While taxis and NYC limousines offer a flat amount for up to 4 persons, airport shuttle buses charge per person (or more for larger limos). Make sure to allow additional time each way because airport shuttles frequently stop along the way to and from the airport. If your group is smaller than four individuals, airport shuttle rates start at about $16 per person and include tolls and round-trip charges, so it's possible you'll save money over the cost of a taxi or limo. However, using JFK as an example, a shuttle will cost $48 and a taxi will cost $70 for 4 persons. It's up to you to decide if an additional hour or two of travel time is worthwhile.

Subway and Bus

For more information than you will ever need on NYC Airports and every last detail on transportation options, see the Wiki Flyer Guide (link:

www.flyerguide.com/wiki/index.php/NYC_Airports_to_Manhattan _Transportation_FAQ) and the NYC Taxi and Limousine Commission (link:

www.nyc.gov/html/tlc/html/passenger/taxicab_rate.shtml). If you choose to take public transit (buses, shuttles, subways), which include several transfers and often carrying your luggage up and down stairs, you can get into NYC from LGA for $2.75, and JFK or EWR for under $10, and the above sites will show you how to do just that.

Save in New York City

It's common knowledge that living in New York City may be expensive, and to some extent, this is true. But whether you're here for a day or a lifetime, there are TONS of ways to save! A true New Yorker knows how to find practically anything at a discount (with the exception of an apartment, a few select events, concerts, and restaurants). Attractions, tours, dinners, Broadway, designer clothing, home furnishings, etc.

City of New York Passes

A first-time tourist to New York City will typically want to check out many of our well-known attractions and may even sign up for numerous excursions. You should compare the New York Sightseeing Pass, New York Pass, New York CityPASS, and New York City Explorer Pass if this is your primary NYC itinerary. Pretty perplexing, huh?

The New York City Pass discounts will save you money in MOST situations, and they frequently come with extra bonuses and discounts around the city as well as a set budget and the ability to avoid lines. The passes conceal a variety of marketing techniques that make them appear to give bigger financial benefits than they actually do. For instance, The Museum of

Modern Art (MoMA) is free on some days and times, while other museums only accept "recommended donations."

FREE Attractions and Museums (Waived Admission)

The list of museums that typically charge entrance fees but don't during specific days and times is shown below.

Mondays, Eldridge Street Museum, 10 a.m. to 5 p.m.

Tuesdays, 9 a.m. to 11 p.m. Memorial Museum

Morgan Library & Museum, McKim rooms, Brooklyn Botanic Garden, 3-5pm

Wave Hill, 9am to 12pm or all day, depending on the season

China Institute Gallery, depending on the season, 6–8pm

Wednesdays, 4–8 p.m., Museum of Jewish Heritage

Pay what you like at the Bronx Zoo; all funds go toward their job caring for animals.

Garden of the NY

Thursdays, 6–9 pm, American Craft Museum (previously the Museum of Arts and Design)

Young People's Museum of the Arts, 4-6pm

a contemporary art museum, 7-9pm

Fridays, 5-8pm, International Center for Photography (ICP), Bronx Museum of the Arts

UNIQLO, MoMA Free Fri., 4–8 p.m.

McKim rooms, Morgan Library & Museum 7 to 9pm

The New York Historical Society accepts donations. 6 to 8 pm

The Whitney Museum of American Art accepts donations. 7-10 pm

Saturdays, 10 a.m. to noon, Brooklyn Botanic Garden

5:45–7:45 p.m. at the Guggenheim

11:00 a.m. to 5:45 p.m. at the Jewish Museum

New York Botanic Garden Access to the grounds is free from 10:00am till 12:00pm

9 a.m. to 12 p.m. Wave Hill

Sunday, Frick Collection from 11:00 to 1:00

Harlem Studio Museum

4 to 6 p.m. at the Morgan Library & Museum's McKim rooms

New York Vacation Budget

How much money do you have to spend in New York City? This definitely depends on your preferences and financial situation, as well as how well you adhere to all of my NYC coupon and discount tips, but here are some broad guidelines and price ranges.

Hotels

In this situation, we're considering 1-4 people in a room because the average hotel pricing in Manhattan is $250-$300 per night, which suggests either one King/Queen bed or two double/Queen beds.

There are always methods to save money or spend more. $1,000 per night for ultra-luxury accommodations. Hotels outside of Manhattan, hostels, and secret offers (like those on HotWire.com, where you aren't told the name of the hotel until you pay) may all have reduced rates. Discount hotels for members of certain groups (religious organizations, charities, the military, etc.), as well as YMCAs and other types of specialized lodging, are available. There are hotels in New York City for every taste and most budgets, with lower rates available for shared bathrooms, bunk beds, and houseboats.

There is also AirBnB, couch surfing, and vacation rentals; but, in New York City, these activities are practically all prohibited, and nothing unlawful is advocated in this book.

Your budget should be around $300 per night per room, including tax, assuming you're looking for a 3–4 star, affordable hotel in Manhattan with a private toilet (13 percent).

Eating and Dining

This is a challenging question because, in reality, daily spending per person can range from $20 to $200. Here are three sample budgets for a typical traveler to New York City; you may always mix and match the various meal options on various days to stick to your own budget.

Basic: $20 per day. This is based on the supposition that you will purchase a street vendor's coffee and bagel for breakfast, a pizza slice and Coke for lunch, and possibly Chinese food in Chinatown for supper.

Medium - $60 per day. Breakfast (omelet, pancakes, or bagel and lox) in a typical NYC diner is $15. Lunch at a classy café or a regular deli in New York ($15–$20). Dinner for two in a reasonable restaurant, with an entrée and possibly tapas, sushi, or nouvelle cuisine ($20–$25 per person). The price of a kid's dinner at any sit-down restaurant should be adjusted by adding

$10 for each drink or glass of wine, 20% gratuity on all meals served, and halving the meal price.

Elegant - $100+ per day. For a normal New Yorker, let's say on a weekend when out with friends and family, this is actually "moderate." Breakfast with Eggs Benedict and unlimited Bloody Marys or Champagne is $20; lunch with a glass of wine at a West Village outdoor café costs $25; and dinner with steak, seafood, or French cuisine costs at least $50. For the cost of a kid's dinner at any sit-down restaurant, add 20% gratuity to all meals provided and halve the meal price.

This excludes the five-star, Michelin-rated restaurants, which will all set you back at least $100 per person and include Per Se, Gramercy Tavern, Peter Lugers, Le Bernadin, and Daniel. The suggested spending amounts are for a typical NYC traveler.

Chapter 3:

Places to Stay And Eat in New York

It's a cliché, but New York truly has something for everyone in terms of dining and lodging. You will undoubtedly find something to adore, regardless of your spending limit or preference. The only challenge you'll face is choosing which restaurant to try in the city. Nevertheless, it provides you with a compelling reason to come back, doesn't it?

However, the hotels frequently include conveniences like WiFi, free tea and coffee, and continental breakfasts. Check the whole pricing list before making a reservation because some locations charge extra for things like linen and luggage storage, which could drive up the cost of that initially low-cost room. You should also be aware that not all hotels have full en-suite bathrooms, and if you're staying in a hostel, you're almost certainly going to have to share.

The tariffs will also depend on the neighborhood where you are staying. Both in terms of hotels and restaurants, SoHo is very upscale. There aren't many deals to be gained because lodging is in high demand year-round due to the location of the art shows. Even though the Upper East Side is pricey, it does have the benefit of being close to Central Park and Museum Mile. There are several excellent, albeit pricey, restaurants here if you want to treat yourself, and the shopping is fantastic if you want to buy high-quality souvenirs.

Times Square and Midtown West may be in the center of the excitement, great for Broadway, and plenty of restaurants ranging from cheap to upscale, but there are two significant drawbacks. First off, you won't get to live like a local and experience New York as it really is since you'll be there with all the other visitors. Additionally, it could be difficult for you to find lodging in the neighborhood, and you won't find any inexpensive lodging options.

Many people view Greenwich Village as the epitome of what New York is all about. This is for you if you enjoy the intimacy of small, meandering streets and if you enjoy soaking up the mood and history of your surroundings. Along with a good selection of pubs, restaurants, and clubs, there is a ton of shopping and entertainment close by. However, especially on weekends, it can become extremely busy and raucous.

Here are some suggestions for accommodations in New York. They will range from inexpensive locations to help you stay within your means to more pricey locations if you want to travel in style. You can pick the option that would allow you and your family to enjoy the city the most.

Andaz Wall Hotel

The 253-room Andaz, a favorite of young professionals in downtown, takes sleek and handsome and gives it a laid-back, new-school air. iPads are used to check guests in, and they are given free Wi-Fi, local calls, and minibar soda and snacks. Oak floors, 7-foot-high windows, and supremely comfy beds with 300-thread-count cotton linens are all features of the rooms, which are also big, modern, and tastefully restrained.

Gild Hall

Gild Hall's entrance is chic and stunning, leading to a split-level lobby that exudes a look best described as "Wall St meets hunting lodge." High tin ceilings, Sferra linens, and well equipped minibars combine European beauty and American comfort in the rooms. Leather headboards for king-size beds look great in their warmly colored, minimalist surrounds.

Greenwich

From the lavish drawing room with a roaring fire and deep armchairs to the lantern-lit pool within a reconstructed 18th-century Japanese farmhouse, Robert De Niro's Greenwich Hotel has nothing in common with other hotels. Each of the 88 individually designed rooms has an aged-wood floor and a magnificent bathroom with Carrara marble or Moroccan tile. French windows in several rooms open onto Tuscan-themed indoor courtyards.

Roxy Hot hotel

In one foxy package, the redesigned Tribeca Grand offers opulent living, mid-century splendor, movies, music, drinking, and dining. The hotel's 201 rooms are arranged around a large central atrium with many bars and are furnished with contemporary fixtures in a vintage brown-and-gold color scheme.

AKA Tribeca

AKA recently acquired this boutique hotel, which provides more than just a sense of Tribeca grandeur. The 100 soundproofed rooms are a relaxing combination of charcoal carpets, walnut paneling, and marble bathrooms with plenty of rain showers, while the lobby, designed by Gachot, has a pleasant, stylish,

Scandinavian atmosphere thanks to the futuristic furniture, rugs, and book-lined shelves. The most expensive rooms have balconies with city views.

Conrad New York

The Hilton group's opulent hotel in Battery Park City is a fantastic choice for business travelers. Loopy Doopy, a large Sol LeWitt mural that climbs the wall of the 15-story atrium, is one of the treasure trove of more than 2000 pieces of art. The 463 suites are elegantly furnished and attractively designed in earthy tones. Prices are lower on the weekends.

THE LOWDOWN ON APARTMENT RENTALS

There are hundreds of alternatives in NYC for travelers looking at home-sharing services, ranging from rooms and studios to penthouse apartments. Private rooms and small studio apartments in Manhattan cost about $100 per night (multi-room apartments might cost several hundred dollars per night), while prices start at $80 in Brooklyn neighborhoods like Clinton Hill and Bed-Stuy. Before clicking "book now," be aware that the Multiple Dwelling Law in New York City makes it illegal to rent out an apartment for less than 30 days unless the host also resides there. However, hosts could face fines (ranging from $1000 to $7500) rather than guests. Travelers are faced with a moral quandary as legal disputes between NYC and Airbnb continue. If you book a desirable short-term apartment rental, you might be adding to the pressure on the NYC housing market, where rents are high and landlords are more and more enticed to make quick money from short-term guests.

Bowery House hostel

This formerly run-down motel from the 1920s has been converted into an upscale hostel with rooms decorated with movie posters from the Bowery and mattresses created to order (i.e., shorter and narrower). Rain showers are available in the public restrooms. There is a bustling bar, a rooftop patio, and a posh living area with chesterfield couches and chandeliers.

As this location draws a crowd who enjoys the nightlife, light sleepers may want to stay away from it; earplugs are provided in every room as standard.

Hotel Hugo

Hotel Hugo is a quiet champion in this expensive neighborhood, despite not having all the bells and whistles of certain SoHo hotels. The rooms have an industrial design, and there is a chic restaurant-cafe and rooftop bar. Even in the height of the tourist season, rates can be as little as $240 per night, so the 10- to 15-minute walk to central SoHo is acceptable.

Nomo SoHo

Neobaroque whimsy highlights the lavish, somewhat small rooms of this gorgeous downtown property, where creamy whites and dreamy blues meet flouncy sconces and marble bathrooms. The upper-level lodgings will give you the sense that you are staring out at Manhattan from a cloud. The front desk of the hotel is upstairs.

Soho Grand hotel

The original boutique hotel in the area still stands out with its stunning glass and cast-iron lobby stairway, 353 rooms with cool, contemporary lines, Frette linens, flat-screen TVs, and unique grooming products. The Grand Bar & Lounge in the foyer is packed with scene-setters and the occasional celebrity. Dog visitors can use the same amenities that are offered to human visitors.

Broome Boutique HOTEL

The Broome seems much more homey than other NYC hotels because it is housed in a beautifully refurbished 19th-century structure. Its 14 rooms, each with locally selected furnishings, are the picture of understated elegance. There's also a secret bonus here: a serene interior terrace with seating in the Parisian style for unwinding with a coffee (which is complimentary, as is the farm-to-table breakfast). The staff here is friendly.

Crosby Street Hotel

This hotel's interior design team defied convention, and the results are stunning. But that's where the similarity of the massive headboards and identical mannequins in the guest rooms ends. With some being starkly black and white and others being as floral as an English garden, all are silky, graceful, and quietly quirky.

Hotel 50 Bowery

This brand-new shop is located right in Chinatown and features luxuriously modern rooms, custom bath products, fine linens, robes with red dragons, and original artwork by NYC-based artists. A hip rooftop bar provides unrivaled city views and is a perfect place to start your on foot tour of Tribeca, SoHo, the Lower East Side, and Brooklyn (across the Manhattan Bridge).

Mercer

Stars snooze at the historic Mercer in the middle of SoHo's cobblestone alleys. In a century-old warehouse, 74 rooms provide a taste of trendy loft living above a lobby filled with large, comfortable armchairs. The rooms have a contemporary feel thanks to the flat-screen TVs, dark hardwood flooring, and white-tiled bathrooms (some with soaking tubs).

James New York

In each of its various spaces, The James plays with a multitude of architectural components, and somehow they all come together nicely. The public spaces combine lots of natural light with amusing accents, such the computer-key mural in the lobby. The straightforward bedrooms upstairs feature reclaimed timber floors, floor-to-ceiling windows, and motorized screens that divide each from its copper-colored bathroom.

The little rooftop plunge pool, replete with sexy bar Jimmy for see-and-be-seen beverages, adds to the sex appeal. In the off-season, prices might drop as low as $250.

St Mark's Hotel

This welcoming establishment attracts a young, cosmopolitan clientele who enjoy the proximity of one of the city's busiest concentrations of bars and restaurants to the front door. Given the low pricing, it's advisable to have lower expectations considering how small the rooms are. For light sleepers, street noise could be a problem. There isn't a lift.

Ludlow Hotel

This boutique hotel with 175 rooms exudes New York elegance. Beautifully constructed rooms have unusual elements like little balconies, petrified tree trunk nightstands, and enormous golden-hued ceiling lights (although the cheapest rooms are quite small). There is a lovely terrace and lobby bar, as well as the well regarded French cafe Dirty French, which is open for breakfast, lunch, and dinner.

Sago Hotel

No matter how hot it is in New York City, the Sago Hotel always appears to be cool. Its location in the bustling center of the Lower East Side and all of the rooms' clean lines, gray masonry, and straightforward contemporary furnishings reflect the neighborhood's current vibe. Terraces with amazing city views are available on the higher levels.

This beaux-arts fantasy, crowned by a copper dome, is one of the city's trendiest destinations. In the rooms' nostalgic New York City/Paris architecture, recycled hardwood floors, minibars constructed of leather steam trunks, and Victorian clawfoot tubs coexist with flat-screen TVs and cutting-edge LED lighting. A well-liked hangout, the hotel's own MoMad restaurant's bar is routinely listed among the World's 50 Best Bars.

Andaz Fifth Avenue

youthful, fashionable The Andaz does away with stuffy front desks in favor of young, active staff who check you in while using laptops in the gallery-like setting of the lobby. The 184 clean, contemporary rooms in the hotel include NYC-inspired details like lighting that resembles subway vehicles and rolling racks from the "Fashion District." Given their proximity to the New York Public Library, the rooms are quiet and roomy for New York (beginning at 320 square feet). Snacks made locally are available in minibars.

Chatwal New York Hotel

In the heart of the Theater District lies the gorgeously restored art deco treasure known as The Chatwal. In the past, famous people like Fred Astaire and Irving Berlin dined, drank, and performed in the structure's former Lambs Club, which had a theater motif. The walls of lavish rooms contain vintage Broadway posters and closets designed to seem like steamer trunks, but they also have contemporary amenities like iPad room controls and TVs built into bathroom mirrors.

The Quin

 is a lavish, contemporary hotel that has the structure of a stately old dame. It was the illustrious Buckingham in the 1920s, which played host to singers and artists like Marc Chagall and Georgia O'Keefe. Today, it maintains the connection to the arts through revolving exhibitions by resident artists and a 15-foot video wall showing projects. Rooms are incredibly cozy and tastefully understated.

Four Seasons

The IM Pei-designed, five-star Four Seasons hotel is housed in a 52-floor structure. The neutrally colored rooms are all amply sized, with roomy closets and HD TVs in the bathrooms with Tuscan marble. The "Park View" rooms at the hotel offer nearly unfair views of Central Park, and the hotel's renowned spa also contributes to the oohs and aahs.

Plaza Hotel

The 282 guest rooms at the renowned Plaza, housed in a historic French Renaissance-style structure, are a royal affair with lavish Louis XV-style furniture and 24-carat gold-plated bathroom faucets. The Guerlain Spa and storied Palm Court, the latter famous for its stained-glass ceiling and afternoon tea, are both on-site attractions. (The hotel's daily $14.95 wi-fi cost is less alluring.)

Iberostar 70 Park

This luxurious hotel provides 205 dazzling rooms with comfortable soft mattresses (including Frette linens) and a palette of rich golds and greys, in addition to a pleasant lobby area with a limestone fireplace. For families, adjoining rooms can be combined to create spacious suites. Pets are welcome, the staff is welcoming, and in-room spa services are available.

Knickerbocker

The 330-room Knickerbocker Hotel, which John Jacob Astor first opened in 1906, emanates a subdued, monochromatic grandeur. The rooms are swanky, quiet, and contemporary, with a 55-inch flat-screen TV that can be adjusted, bedside tablet and USB charging points, and Carrara-marble bathrooms. Inside, the triple-glazed windows maintain a beautiful sense of calm, yet the building's Times Square location results in constant mayhem immediately outside the front door.

Hotel Ink48

With Ink48, positioned on the outer reaches of Manhattan without any subway access, the Kimpton hotel chain has braved the wild west of Midtown. Being located in a former printing house, the compensation is sweet: amazing views of the skyline and the Hudson River, sleek, modern rooms, a quaint spa and restaurant, and a spectacular rooftop bar. The vibrant restaurant scene in Hell's Kitchen is easily accessible on foot, which is the cherry on top.

The complimentary bowl of food and water immediately outside the foyer will be appreciated by dog owners (pets stay for free). Wi-Fi, free local and long distance calls, and a $10 daily food credit for the hotel's on-site restaurant are all included in the daily $30 amenities fee.

New York's Muse

The Kimpton company, known for its boutique hotels, is providing you with The Muse, a dazzling 200-room high-rise adjacent to the theater district.

Recent renovations have given their rooms striking black dcor, Frette linens, and pop art touches. Additionally, there are free bike rentals, an evening wine reception, and in-room spa treatments available. The personnel is generally polite.

The daily $30 amenities fee includes Wi-Fi and a $10 bar credit.

Hotel Lowell

Despite having 74 rooms, this chic boutique hotel feels considerably smaller due to its location off Madison Avenue on a residential street lined by trees. When it first made its debut as an apart-hotel in 2017, intimacy now predominates after being refurbished by Obama White House designer Michael Smith. Some of the rooms have working fireplaces and contemporary marble-tiled bathrooms, and the decor is understated with beige and grey accents.

Nest bamboo emits a powerful perfume that fills the entire space. Because it provides windows with a clear view of the 63rd Street treeline, the fourth floor is preferred by the majority of individuals. The upcoming Belgian chef Emmanuel Niess has improved the cuisine at the traditional French fine-dining Majorelle, which is well worth a classy evening out (two/three/five courses $105/122/155). It also has a lovely library and a hot bar (Jacques). The Lowell has received the Travel+Leisure World's Best Awards two years running for best hotel in New York City chosen by readers.

Hotel Mark Design

French designer Jacques Grange's creative influence can be seen throughout The Mark, where the lobby's vibrant geometric shapes and rich, whimsical forms greet visitors (the zebra-striped marble floor, which carries on to the room bathrooms, is pure eye candy). Upstairs, the elegantly remodeled rooms and multi-bedroom suites are as lavish, with extras like exquisite local linens and custom-made furniture.

Hotel Loews Regency

Park Avenue shoppers flock to this legendary hotel. Even at the nearby Bloomingdales, guests receive 15% off (and 25% off during the holidays). The hotel's interior is intended to resemble an apartment building in the Upper East Side. Its 379 rooms, which range in size from 325 to 375 square feet on average, feature spacious workspaces and gorgeous marble bathrooms with professional-style hair dryers. There are balconies in some rooms.

Hostelling International New York

This 1880s red-brick mansion is home to the 734 bunk beds at HI. Despite having a rather 19th-century industrial exterior, it offers good public areas, a backyard (where barbecues are commonly used in the summer), a communal kitchen, a cafe, and other ecologically friendly projects. There are lots of options, from club nights to walking expeditions. The receptionists can be troublesome, and there is a staffing deficit.

Three nice private rooms with private bathrooms are offered. Alcohol is not available at the hostel.

HOSTEL YMCA

Simple but immaculate rooms, the most of which have shared bathrooms, are located on the eighth through twelfth floors of this magnificent art deco building, which is only a few steps from Central Park. Several recently renovated doubles include en suite bathrooms on floors 12 and 13. Visitors have access to a spacious, historic gym with racquetball courts, a pool, and a sauna.

Four other YMCAs, including ones in Midtown, the Upper East Side, and Harlem, are nearby and offer housing.

NYC Arthouse Hotel

Modern industrial design and antique furniture are combined in this boutique hotel with a focus on art. Visitors can unwind in the stylish lounge and bar rooms on the ground level after a day of sightseeing. The 291 bright rooms up top have lots of natural light and elegant décor. Coffeemakers, flat-screen TVs, and marble bathrooms are contemporary amenities that complement mid-century design elements.

There is also a public outdoor terrace on the 16th floor that occasionally hosts pop-up bars if you can't afford the penthouse residences. These suites provide spectacular views of Manhattan and equipped own terraces. Following a recent renovation, the hotel lobby's Warhols and Basquiats will cohabit with pieces from Upper West Side artists.

Inn Beacon

This establishment is a family favorite because it combines friendly service, comfortable lodging, and a terrific location just near to the Beacon Theatre. The Beacon's 278 rooms, some of which include several bedrooms, are decorated in muted Pottery Barn green tones. The large, immaculate flats all come with kitchenettes and coffeemakers. The amenities include a bar, a gym, outdoor cycling lessons, and self-service laundry.

The highest stories on the east side of the skyscraper have distant views of Central Park. It's a wonderful deal, and off-season bargains often provide large discounts.

Belleclaire Hotel

The classic beaux-arts building designed by Emory Roth, completed in 1903, has a 249-room hotel with reasonable rates for the neighborhood. Modern, vibrant spaces exist in a variety of shapes and configurations, some larger or with more natural light than others. Full (double) to king-sized beds are available. There are internal tunnels in certain rooms, so be mindful of that.

Empire Hotel

Just across the street from Lincoln Center, the ancient Empire is now reduced to its skeletal remains.

A canopied pool deck, a sizable Empire Rooftop bar, and a seductive two-story lobby area with a sweeping staircase and floor-to-ceiling draperies have all been added as a result of extensive renovations. Its 420 rooms include comfortable dark-leather furnishings and walls painted in vibrant hues.

Flophouse in Harlem

Relive the Harlem Jazz Age in this quaint 1890s townhouse's four evocative rooms, each with brass beds and antique radios. There are no televisions, air conditioners, or private facilities since it seems like stepping back in time. One of the downstairs lounges doubles as a music area where sporadic small concerts are held.

The warm, welcoming ambiance is completed by Phoebe, the friendly house cat. For extended visits, the owner also provides a sizable basement suite ($175/night; contact personally) with a double bed, a single bed, and an ensuite bathroom.

Aloft Hotel in Harlem

The elegant Aloft maintains affordable prices while appealing to younger travellers. Despite being compact (285 square feet), the guest rooms are attractive and feature spotless white linens, thick comforters, and eye-catching striped bolsters. The elegant Bliss spa chain equipped the modest, extremely functional modern bathrooms, which are small and devoid of bathtubs.

Even though the basement bar with pool tables is far from your room, it can get noisy there. In addition to being in close proximity to the Apollo Theater and the bustling 125th Street business district, Aloft is a fantastic value.

Bed and Breakfast Lefferts Manor

This traditional Brooklyn brownstone's six bright rooms with historically inspired furnishings, tiled closed fireplaces, and soft color schemes. The Parlor Suite includes a private toilet and a clawfoot tub, while the other five rooms share two sparkling white bathrooms. Usually, there are minimum stays required, but if you inquire, one-night trips can be permitted ($30 cost). continental breakfast is optional. strictly for adults.

The owners also have rooms available in two adjoining properties with similar amenities, as well as two flats in Fort Greene with complete kitchens.

The subway ride to downtown Manhattan takes just 30 minutes.

Hotel NY Moore

NY Moore, which is covered in murals both inside and out, fits in perfectly in this gritty East Williamsburg neighborhood. Women-only dorms and private triples are two sizes of tidy dorm rooms that are available. There is a large kitchen as well as a baroque-style lounge and business center as benefits. It seems safe and welcoming at the same time thanks to the 24-hour reception and the pleasant employees.

Pod hotel in Brooklyn

Although the rooms are small, the hotel's facilities are crammed into small places, including wet-room shower toilets, retractable clothes hangers, and safes under the beds. Excellent for single travelers and couples looking for a modern sleep pad; less comfortable for tall people. For more space, go to the rooftop bar or simply go outside to the pubs and restaurants in the heart of Williamsburg.

The L Hotel

The L Hotel's well-kept, small rooms have comfortable beds, complementary breakfast, writing desks, showers with adequate water pressure, and helpful reception personnel, although the soundproofing could be improved and the decor is a little antiquated. The L won't make your vacation but it ain't half bad if you're looking for a reasonably priced hotel that's five minutes' walk from the metro.

Hotel Henry Norman

This beautiful brick building, which originally housed artist lofts, is situated in a former 19th-century warehouse and is designed in a manner resembling a love letter to Brooklyn. With hardwood flooring, dove-gray sofas, brass lamps, and vibrant artwork around the high-ceilinged rooms that were all created by the same Brooklyn artist, they have a bohemian but sartorial feel.

Look through the website for discounts for reservations.

Hotel McCarren & Pool

The main draw of this posh hotel with mural-covered walls is the tropical-style pool area, where clients throw themselves across lounge chairs while holding cocktails. The majority of the rooms have balconies, and they are decorated like a cool friend's living room with velvet sofas, vinyl records, and the occasional guitar. A rooftop vegan restaurant and jazz bar let you start your evening right there. The pool is only open during the summer.

Wythe Inn

The red-brick Wythe (pronounce "white") Hotel, located in a former factory that was transformed in 1901, adds a touch of high design to Williamsburg. 13-foot timber ceilings and exposed brick allow the building's past to breathe. Reclaimed wood beds, a subtly nautical theme, vintage paisley, leather, and custom wallpaper all work together to create a place that is both rustic and exquisite.

Homes Located in Brooklyn

Inside an upscale Brooklyn address is a guesthouse with a very sophisticated aesthetic. Each room is elegantly furnished with painted armoires, wicker chairs, and rugs in addition to premium double and king-sized mattresses. The communal areas are filled with books, and a dapper host greets guests and prepares a great continental breakfast dish. Pleasantly placed on Prospect Park's northern border.

Brooklyn Borough

If customers are unbothered by its dismal location close to a bustling main road, The Brooklyn is a beautiful, boutique hotel that delivers great luxury for the price. There are large rooms with contemporary bare-brick, tall ceilings, and accent walls celebrating Brooklyn business. The bathrooms are spacious and spa-like, and the beds are as comfy as clouds. Online reservations made in advance might save you a lot of money.

Hotel EVEN

EVEN wants its guests to feel revitalized, which is why there is lemon-mint water at the front desk and workout equipment in each room. Every area has yoga mats, stability balls, color-changing lights, and fitness videos. The emphasis on fitness is maintained with the 24-hour gym and nutritious breakfast choices including avocado-egg wraps ($10).

The metro stops are incredibly accessible due to Downtown Brooklyn's central position.

NU Hotel

The rooms at NU have industrial style thanks to Brooklyn-themed accents, repurposed teak furniture, and occasionally eyebrow-raising artwork. Free bikes are a useful amenity, and the location, on the border between Boerum Hill and Downtown, is convenient. The "Bunkbed" suite, which has a queen bed and twin bunk beds, is a good option for groups of four. Art enthusiasts will like the "NU Perspective" rooms' mural-covered walls.

Winton Garden Park Sunset in Brooklyn

This charming chain hotel is situated between two lush green local landmarks, Sunset Park and Green-Wood Cemetery, and offers welcoming, modern rooms and competent front desk personnel. A calming atmosphere is created with flashes of moss green and frosted glass, and more expensive "executive" suites provide views of the Manhattan skyline. So make reservations in advance to take advantage of early-bird and online discounts.

Hotel Williamsburg

This eight-story, industrial-chic hotel is situated just two blocks from the water and enjoys breathtaking views of the river and Manhattan. The "terrace" rooms on the north side are worth the extra cost because they provide a continuous view of the Chrysler Building, the Upper East Side, and the Empire State Building from your artificial-grass-carpeted balcony (some have swing chairs).

Smallish rooms appear more spacious because to floor-to-ceiling windows and glassed-in baths with vibrant subway tiles. Standard facilities include minibars, leather headboards, safes, and essential-oil products made locally by Apotheke. There includes a rooftop bar modeled after a vintage New York City water tower (open Wednesday through Saturday from 6 p.m. to 4 a.m.), an outdoor rooftop pool, and free pushbikes for exploring Williamsburg.

Hotel Aloft New York

Outside of the steely grey industrial-style lobby, the Aloft's rooms have leatherette couches, flat-screen TVs, great beds, and walls covered in old photos of Brooklyn. The rooms also have flat-screen TVs. Everything is little yet snug and contemporary, from the breakfast bar (which has cold brew on tap) to the rooftop terrace.

Cobble Hill and Fort Greene's restaurants and nightlife are nearby. Parking off-site is accessible and costs $65 per day.

Local hostel

The Local offers neat, lovely en-suite doubles and dorms, making it an excellent low-cost lodging option (male, female, and mixed, all with under-bed storage). The café converts into a bar at night, there is frequently an evening event, and whimsical art is placed next to the reception area. The kitchen is well-equipped (movie nights, live music, pub quizzes).

Some of New York City's lesser-known gems will be pointed out by the friendly staff. Don't forget to enjoy the scenery while on the rooftop, which is the site of summer DJ performances.

Hotel Boro

For a lot less than you would pay in Manhattan, The Boro delivers minimalist city elegance (high-quality linens, luxurious robes, tubs in the suites), plus the added bonus of brilliant skyline views from the floor-to-ceiling windows. The rooms have hardwood flooring and high ceilings, and some standards come with patio areas. There is a fitness center, and the continental breakfasts are above average, including fluffy croissants and Greek yogurt.

HOSTELS Q4

It's difficult to argue against this basic hostel covered in Keith Haring-inspired paintings because it's inexpensive, clean, and close to the train. It doesn't have a phone (very millennial!) and the elevated train that passes by in front can make the rooms a little shaky. The number of beds in dorm rooms ranges from two (excellent) to eight (squeezed); private queen rooms are a possibility.

Hotel TWA

Far be it from us to suggest that you visit NYC and stay at JFK (but that's exactly what we're about to do!). The famed neo-futurist Eero Saarinen's iconic 1962 TWA Flight Center has been converted into a one-of-a-kind, LEED-certified hotel that screams Gilded Age of Travel.

There are too many noteworthy features and specifics to list them all in full. Connie, a 1958 Lockheed Constellation propeller-driven, four-engine airliner that once transported drugs to Colombia but is now a creative cocktail bar, and one of NYC's coolest pools— a rooftop plane-spotter haven with views of runways 4L and 22R—represent the pinnacle of retro-hipster-traveler craziness. Public day passes range in price from $25 to $50. It also serves as a virtual museum: ancient TWA artifacts are displayed in a few spots, old Solari split-flaps display flight information, Saarinen's womb chairs, tulip lamps, and tables can be found everywhere, and minibars tempt with items from the 1960s (Sugar Daddies, TAB sodas, mini Etch A Sketches). Saarinen's incredible right angle-free architecture, Intelligentsia coffee, Jean-Georges Vongerichten's Paris Café, and the world's largest hotel fitness center round out this trip back in time.

A time window can be selected (7am to 11am, 10am to 4pm, noon to 6pm for $149; 8am to 8pm for $209) or a night can be reserved.

Rockaway Camp

From Memorial Day until October 15, this temporary pop-up glamping site on Riis Beach in the Jacob Riis bathhouse courtyard serves as a dreamy beach getaway from the Big Apple. On elevated wood platforms that extend to give a deck and two chairs, safari-style canvas tents are set up. A picnic area, a camp store, hammocks, games, and a shared fire pit are available amenities.

Hotel The Collective Paper Factory

This five-story Long Island City structure, which was formerly a radio factory (paper arrived later), is now home to a whimsical jewel of a hotel after undergoing a complete renovation in 2021.

The industrial-chic accommodations have a touch of refinement and feature modern mattresses, decent showers, and vintage movie props from the personal collection of the former owner without sacrificing comfort.

Z Hotel NYC

Under the iconic Silvercup Studios sign, among the industrial alleyways, this chic tower provides comfortable lodging and amazing views of Manhattan. The extra-large showerheads and heated bathroom floors are nice extras. The 100 renovated rooms are compact yet lovely, decorated in deep purple. There is a basement cocktail bar with a restricted menu, and discounted accommodations can be found online.

With an additional mandatory "Experience Fee" of $30, guests receive free Manhattan transit (perhaps shifting to subway station only in the future), an enhanced continental breakfast, free Wi-Fi, free international phone calls, and, in good weather, free bike rental.

Wolcott Hotel

This landmark hotel in the heart of Manhattan dates back more than a century. Additionally well-known guests have included Mark Twain and Buddy Holly more recently. Starting at $125 a night, fully equipped rooms include with Internet connectivity in case you need to work or meet up with friends. If guests desire to work out, they are welcome to use the hotel's complimentary fitness center. Nearby attractions include Theatreland, Macy's, the United Nations headquarters, and the Empire State Building.

But the experience is not only about the lodging. You'll want a wonderful, laid-back restaurant to dine after a long day of soaking in New York's sights, sounds, and smells. You could also just want to go out and party. New York has several great dining options to offer, whether you're looking for a cheap diner or a classy dining experience.

This is one of the best locations to go if you want to eat well and at a renowned restaurant worldwide. Your pals will all be jealous of you because you get to go there, and you can learn a lot about history from it. Make your reservations in advance to ensure a smooth arrival and a delicious lunch.

The roughly 20,000 eateries in New York cater to every taste, but it might be a touch confusing for first-time tourists who haven't had time to make a "hit list" of restaurants. Here are some ideas for where to dine while touring New York.

HI-New York

With 672 beds and rates starting at $60 per night, HI (Hosteling International) is the biggest hostel in North America. On the Upper West Side, the hostel is advantageously located close to Columbia University, Broadway, Central Park, and a significant subway line. The hostel provides visitors with a variety of activities, such as several walking tours, which range in price from $10 per person to free, depending on the tour. There are also entertainment nights inside the hostel, as well as planned outings to bars and clubs where hostel guests can benefit from free or discounted entrance and drink specials. As a result, your visit will be much more memorable because you will be practically blending in.

You may find hostels to be a wonderful and cozy destination. While they are well-liked in Europe and offer all the contemporary comforts you want when you want to feel comfortable, they are not as well-liked in America as they are in other nations. These are popular options because they are extremely affordable, especially considering that they are located in the city and are so close to numerous attractions that you can walk to many of them.

Radio City Apartments

This Manhattan hotel is made up of apartments, each of which has a kitchenette, making it the perfect choice for families or couples who enjoy some freedom and the ability to prepare drinks whenever they please. Although it costs a bit extra each bed—roughly $80—it is conveniently located near Times Square, the Rockefeller Center, Fifth Avenue stores, and the Theatre District. It's the perfect starting point for seeing New York because the renowned Radio City Music Hall is nearby and the subway is conveniently located.

This is the finest place for you to stay if you are bringing a big group of people or intend to stay in the city for a while. It is more inexpensive than some of the other hotel options, but it will feel more like home. You will have plenty of space to move around in and your own place that you won't have to share with some of the other people. You will also be able to prepare some of your own meals if you so desire. It is also close to many of the New York City attractions you'll want to see, so you won't have to worry about commuting while on vacation.

Food trucks

If you're visiting New York for a brief period of time or are on a limited budget, you might want to try some of the city's well-known food trucks. America has had food trucks since 1691, back when New York was still known as New Amsterdam. They now sell food that is on par with what you would find at a restaurant. Everything is accessible for consumption on the go, from a bagel or pizza slice to a grass-fed Aberdeen Angus hamburger with all the fixings.

Three substantial or healthful meals are offered by the many food trucks dotted across the various neighborhoods. Unsure of what to choose or where to look for the best food carts? Join the Gourmet Food Cart Walking Tour on Wednesdays and Fridays to sample six of the best food cart experiences and learn more about the neighborhood from your friendly guide. Starting prices are $48.

The annual Food Truck Rally takes place in Brooklyn's Prospect Park on the third Sunday of every month from April through October. Go there if you're in the city at that time. You have a large range of takeout options if you go to the park during the Rally. Then why not love it?

Eating from a food truck is an experience you won't be able to find in every city you visit. If you are from a small town somewhere else, visiting a food truck when you are in the city might be fun. You would not anticipate it, but there is a ton of interesting food there.

Before you purchase anything from a food truck, though, be sure to check out the area. Usually, you can tell if it's a good place to stop just by taking a quick glance at it. Select only those that seem to be clean and able to provide you with a filling dinner. To find the best offer, do a little research as well. When you shop around, you can sometimes find similar food trucks with different prices for what you want, which will help you save even more money on your trip. You don't want to spend a lot of money on food that ultimately gets your family ill.

Lunch and dinner cruises

What better place than the Hudson River to enjoy lunch or dinner on a magnificent cruise ship while admiring Manhattan? For supper, dress a little more formally and leave the jeans, shoes, and shorts at home. For lunch, casual wear is OK. The excellent lunch service features a wide variety of vegetarian options. Enjoy the views of the cityscape and the Statue of Liberty while dining on the air-conditioned ship and taking advantage of all the amenities available there. The lunch and dinner cruises are a unique chance to experience fine cuisine while getting a unique perspective of New York. From the ocean, you see things in such various ways.

Lunch and supper start at $51 and $94 respectively depending on the day of the week and whether the cruise is themed or not. These expenses can be reduced with the New York Pass, which will result in substantial long-term savings for you.

Try these if you want to experience something unique when visiting New York. When you're at home, you can dine out whenever you want, so make the most of the chance to board a boat, see some of New York City as you eat, and have a blast that you won't soon forget.

Cheap restaurants in New York

Even if you have a limited budget, you can still eat well in New York thanks to the large variety of eateries. If you want soul cuisine but are on a limited budget, check out Charles' Country Pan-fried Chicken in Harlem. Harlem is a must-see when in New York, and the all-you-can-eat buffet costs $10.99 for lunch and $13.99 for dinner. Charles Gabriel prepares his mother's recipe for approximately 600 chicken pieces per day and 1500 on weekends at one of the few remaining Harlem restaurants providing authentically traditional soul food. Despite the basic setting, the food is superb.

Inexpensive bar food and cheap beverages are available at The Commodore in Williamsburg, Brooklyn, but the quality is everything but cheap. Prices range from $3 to $10, and some reviews have referred to it as offering "the greatest inexpensive pub food in town." Fried chicken and biscuits are the house specialty, and they also provide burgers, pulled pork sandwiches, and hearty stews. Although it is a little loud and obnoxious, there are quieter booths available.

Go to the Gangjong Kitchen in Jackson Heights, Queens, for the least expensive Tibetan and Indian food anyplace in New York. Even the greatest appetites will be satisfied by a three-course supper of soup, salad, curry, and beverages, which can be purchased for as low as $20 for two people. Thukpa, a beef-crumbled noodle soup, is essentially a meal in and of itself.

Planning out the majority of your meals with budget eating in mind is a smart idea. If you don't have a strategy when it comes to eating out in the city, it may get pricey, but if you do, you can find some inexpensive restaurants and significantly reduce your spending if you do.

Before beginning, many people will develop a list of the restaurants they want to eat at. When they are in the city, they will make a list of their day and nightly plans in order to cut costs on their dining out. Look at some of the above possibilities as well as some of your own that have some local flair to show how fantastic your vacation can be on a little budget. There are plenty of cheap restaurants that have a lot of flavors.

Dining in style in New York

There are numerous Michelin-starred eateries in New York, and some of the most well-known celebrity chefs in the world are based there. You won't have any trouble obtaining exquisite dining experiences during your visit as long as your cash is bottomless. However, because the top restaurants are sometimes booked months in advance, you might have trouble getting a reservation. To avoid disappointment, reserve a specific location if you have one in mind as soon as your travel dates are set.

Eleven Madison Park in Flatiron is at the top of most people's lists for great dining in New York City. The restaurant is reputed by some to be the top fine dining establishment in New York, and Business Insider recently ranked it the best restaurant in America. It has critics, of course; doesn't every restaurant? However, this is the place to go if you want a leisurely gourmet dining experience and your wallet can handle the strain. Plan on spending at least three hours for the meal, which consists of a 15-course tasting menu made with as many locally sourced products as possible. With cocktails added on top, this will cost you $225, so budget for a total of at least $800.

The menu features a lot of seafood, including oysters, lobster, foie gras pate, and pig. The welcoming, experienced staff will actually offer you everything you can think of. If you enjoy eating, don't miss the opportunity.

Since 1837, the venerable Delmonico's in the Financial District has served delectable steaks, and author F. Scott Fitzgerald has written about it. Although a steak costs $45 here, the exceptional quality and ambiance make up for the pricey pricing. Seafood is also quite good at Delmonico's.

Mareo in Central Park South is the place to go if you want Italian cuisine. Oysters, antipasto, pasta, meat or fish, and dessert are among the southern Italian coastal dishes included in their four-course tasting menu, which costs $99 per person. Owner and chef Michael White is the proud owner of two Michelin stars and prepares all of his own pasta in the kitchen.

Make sure to set aside at least a portion of your spending money while you are in New York City so that you can dine at one of the upscale eateries that are located in these regions. They have some of the best food in the world and are very amazing. When visiting New York City, you don't have to go out every night to one of these locations, but you should set aside one night and some of your cash to go to one of them as a gift for yourself and to sample something that is absolutely different and great.

Chapter 4:
Places To Visit

Most people see Manhattan when they think of New York. Manhattan, one of the five boroughs in the city proper, offers more fantastic eateries and nightclubs than there are stars in the northern sky. Five of the top 50 ranked fine dining places worldwide are located in Manhattan. Eleven Madison is undoubtedly the top-ranked team this year.

There are enough films, theaters, and Off-Broadway plays and musicals on the "Great White Way" (Broadway) to satisfy any taste. The place to be if you enjoy "shopping 'til you drop" is Manhattan. The best in modern clothing may be found at Saks Fifth Avenue, Lord & Taylor, Neiman Marcus, and Bergdorf Goodman. The opulent shopping experiences in Manhattan can only be matched in Paris or London.

Dutch trader Peter Minuit bought the territory that is now known as Manhattan from a nearby Indian tribe for $24 worth of glass beads, the most unfair transaction in human history. However, some historians believe that the trade was actually valued roughly 69 Dutch Guilders, which is equivalent to $1,100 in modern money. While that was a nice sum in 1626, there are currently 1.7 million people living in Manhattan on property valued roughly $2 billion. That is a fantastic return on your investment.

Uptown

Upper West Side, Morningside Heights, Hamilton Heights, Sugar Hill, Hudson Hill, Harlem, Upper Eastside, and Lenox Hill are all included in the region above 59th Street.

1. visit Central Park.

Take a pleasant, unhurried stroll through this storied green haven in Uptown to kick off your trip to the Big Apple. You will be protected from the roaring trucks and honking sea of yellow taxis outside the park by this serene, leisurely journey. 59th Street borders the Park's southern boundary.

Additionally, you can rent a vintage horse-drawn carriage and enjoy a leisurely journey through the park. The park's southeast corner, next to the Plaza Hotel, is typically where the carriages gather. Request that the carriage driver stop at the Sheep Meadow, Conservatory Garden, Bow Bridge on the Lake, and Belvedere Castle. If time allows, you'll also appreciate a change of pace with a side trip to the Central Park Zoo.

2. Grab a bite to eat at Tavern on the Green.

Following your carriage ride and promenade, stop for a quick lunch at this iconic eatery. The Tavern, located on the western edge of Central Park, serves intriguing food including roasted figs, maple-grilled smoked bacon, and organic Scottish salmon.

3. Pay a visit to the Lincoln Center for the Arts.

Lincoln Center, which John D. Rockefeller founded in 1950, is known across the world for its avant-garde productions of ballet, modern music, drama, film, and symphonies. The complex houses the David Geffen Philharmonic Hall, Main Hall, and an arts library. Anybody who actually enjoys music and dance can find something to cheer them up at one of the 21 venues.

Make sure to reserve seats for captivating productions like A Chorus Line, Swan Lake, or a number of summer dance revues.

4. Attend an old opera.

Although it is connected to the Lincoln Center, the Metropolitan Opera House specializes in opera and classical music. The Met is the largest repertory opera house in the world, with 3,800 seats. This theater also takes pride in possessing cutting-edge stage equipment like hydraulic lifts, mechanized staging, and automatic rigging systems that enable lavish presentations that are unmatched by most operas.

Among other important performances, The Met has staged a number of legendary operas, including Madam Butterfly, Aida, La bohème, and War and Peace.

Definitely a dark suit and tie operation. Ladies should dress elegantly for the evening. During the pre-show party, you can mingle with the local glitterati while sipping costly champagne in the opulent foyer. Even just watching this influential bunch interact is worth the admission price. Few nights in your life will be as unforgettable as this one.

5. Pay a visit to Juilliard.

The most prestigious institution of its kind in the entire globe is The Juilliard School of Music. Juilliard has produced many of the outstanding performers you see on Broadway, in the movies, and on television.

It will astound you to learn that Juilliard alumni have together won 106 Grammys, 62 Tonys, 47 Emmys, 24 Oscars, 16 Pulitzers, and 12 National Medals for the Arts. A partridge in a pear tree, too. Juilliard offers daily tours, so be sure to schedule some time to stop by this outstanding establishment. While they're still affordable, get some autographs from the stars of the future!

6. Take a stroll around the Natural History Museum.

One of the largest museums in the world is housed in this incredible collection of 28 interconnected structures. More than 34 million specimens of rocks, animals, fossils, and plants are kept there. A section on human artifacts and the development of homo sapien culture is also included. Do not overlook the AMNH; it draws more than five million people each year.

7. Have lunch at the Café at the Boat Basin.

The best casual dining can be found at this fantastic eatery. You may enjoy a wonderful supper while admiring the renowned Hudson River. You may eat in the quaint dining room or on the airy porch close to the harbor thanks to the interior design and architecture of the establishment. This café is a great place to take a break from your thorough exploration of Uptown and refresh.

8. Visit Columbia University.

Anyone who visits this prestigious Ivy League university will undoubtedly be impressed by its revered halls. The campus is a tranquil haven in this busy Uptown area.

It will take you on a quick tour of the Law School and Butler Library. Wander over to Bernard College, which is right across Broadway, if you have time. Columbia draws intelligent tourists.

9.The Columbia Wine Company offers wine tastings.

It's time to toast your graduation from Columbia with a beautiful glass of wine. A few kilometers straight north on Broadway will bring you to this fantastic wine shop. The CWC boasts a sizable collection of excellent wines from all over the globe. From Australia to Zimbabwe, reds, whites, and Sauternes are available. Purchase a few bottles of wine after some wine tasting to savor later while watching the city from your hotel window.

10. Visit Marcus Garvey Park and Harlem.

East down 125th Street in old Harlem, starting at Broadway. The hub of African-American trade and culture is this historic area of Manhattan. It's a terrific spot to observe people and take in the unique character of these areas. Afro-Cuban music's rhythmic pulse may be heard bouncing off the colorfully painted walls. Watch neighborhood kids have fun in the priceless patch of greenery that is Markus Garvey Park.

11. Go to the conservancy for the Gracie Mansion.

Since Fiorello Laguardia, one of the most renowned mayors of the city, moved into this gorgeous timber palace in 1942, it has been known as New York's "Little White House," the residence of the mayors of New York City.

These grounds offer unrivaled views of the bay formed by the confluence of the East and Harlem Rivers and are a wonderful haven of peace and nature. Only Tuesday reservations are accepted, so make yours early.

12. Take in the Museum Mile's splendor.

There aren't many cities with as many museums and galleries as New York. This area of property on the Upper East Side is the best illustration of that fact. Multi-million dollar townhouses can be found here, along with the Neue Galerie, the Cooper Hewitt Design Museum, the Jewish Museum, the Guggenheim, and the Metro Art Museum, which are all located along Fifth Avenue between 80th and 93rd Street. In this diverse neighborhood, you will undoubtedly take in a significant amount of art and culture.

13. Wander through the Guggenheim Museum.

Visit this museum without a doubt if you only have the time or energy for one. This must-see building on 88th Street, designed by Frank Lloyd Wright, boasts a distinctive circular exterior design and top-notch artwork. Nowhere in the world, let alone in

America, can you discover a more revered collection of modern, impressionist, or post-impressionist art. Purchase tickets, preferably in advance, but you must do so. Leave New York without having seen it.

14. Go to the Met.

Choose this museum as your sole stop on Museum Mile. The Metropolitan Museum of Art is the biggest art museum in the entire United States, not to be confused with the Met Opera House. Over two million works of art are contained in its collection, which is divided into seventeen categories. The Met is a notable art gallery that you won't soon forget.

One of the biggest art galleries in the entire globe is Just the Main Gallery. Even though The Cloisters is a little bit smaller, it nonetheless has a sizable collection of medieval European artwork, buildings, and artifacts. African, Egyptian, Asian, and Indian artwork and antiques make up the remainder of this magnificent structure. The Henri Matisse exhibition at the Met is wonderful, you will be astounded by the works of other famous artists like Picasso and El Greco.

15. View a performance at the Park Avenue Armory.

The Armory is a trendy place where "starving artists" can perform. It enables emerging artists, visionaries, and art students to exhibit unorthodox performing arts pieces that aren't appropriate for more pricey venues like Broadway or the Met. Many Juilliard students can have their first genuine stage experience at The Armory in front of an attentive New York audience.

Midtown

the region that includes Hell's Kitchen, Sutton Place, the Garment District, 5th Avenue Shopping, and the Diamond District and is located between 34th and 59th Streets.

15. Arrive at Carnegie Hall.

A New Yorker was once asked by a tourist where to find Carnegie Hall. The wise guy answered, "Practice, practice, practice."

The primary concert venue in Manhattan is Carnegie Hall. This theater, which was built in 1891 by the multibillionaire philanthropist Andrew Carnegie, is one of the most prominent stages in America for both classical and popular music. With 3,671 seats split among three exquisite auditoriums, Carnegie hosts roughly 400 concerts, dance performances, and piano recitals annually.

17. Arrange a tour of Fifth Avenue's shops.

Stride southeast toward Fifth Avenue and 59th Street. Pass the Plaza Hotel before exploring Trump Tower's chic boutiques on 57th Street. Along Fifth Avenue, there are many shops to browse while marveling at the unbelievable pricing.

But if you want to make the most of this intimidating journey, scheduling a guided shopping tour is advised. With the help of a knowledgeable guide, you will spend three hours touring all the top high-end boutiques and learning about New York's fashion scene. Don't panic, you still have time to purchase all your budget will allow.

18. Offer up a prayer in Saint Patrick's Cathedral.

This magnificent Catholic building, which first opened its doors in 1879, is a striking example of New York's rich religious and cultural past. Numerous marriages and burials for well-known American politicians, statesmen, and celebrities have taken place at the church. St. Patrick's will serve as a peaceful respite from the busy world that surrounds it. Make a gift and say a little prayer. Your spirit will be revived.

19. Tour the United Nations.

At St. Patrick's, I hope you prayed for world peace because the UN clearly needs all the assistance it can get. Shortly after World War II, the UN was established in 1945 to replace the disastrous League of Nations. Today, there are 193 members, up from 51 when it first started. Among its various duties, the UN performs admirable work on behalf of the UNESCO World Heritage agency, which recognizes and protects significant historic and cultural sites all around the world, many of which you have the honor of visiting.

Visit this wonderful collection of institutions and agencies; it's worth a day. A magnificent tour in six languages will be provided for you, complete with video headsets and an informed guide. This is a fantastic chance to learn.

20. Go to Times Square.

Between 42nd and 47th Streets on Broadway, the Great White Way is located. It is home to the nation's densest concentration of movie theaters, dining establishments, Broadway shows, bars, enormous electronic billboards, and Off-Broadway productions. The astounding sights and noises in Times Square captivate the more than 55 million visitors who come here each year.

21. Attend the Broadway performance of Hamilton.

One of the most well-liked Broadway musicals may be the only one you get to see. One of the Founding Fathers of the United States and George Washington's first Secretary of the Treasury, Alexander Hamilton, is the subject of this magnificent play. The play is fresh, contemporary, and groovy despite the fact that it is based on an old tale.

ask your hotel's concierge for assistance rather than attempting to purchase tickets online. They are in the know and can secure you the greatest seats thanks to their connections. The nicer the seats, the larger the tip. It's New York, hey!

22. Enjoy a meal at Le Bernardin

A magnificent three-star Michelin restaurant that was relocated from Paris to 51st Street and 7th Avenue in 1972. Le Bernardin is the restaurant for you if your budget will accommodate it and you enjoy excellent seafood served in a luxurious setting. Try the Manila clams, wild mushroom casserole, or the poached halibut. However, reservations are required for lunch and supper, so don't just show up.

23.Visit Rockefeller Center

A terrific area to shop, eat a hot dog, enjoy some delicious ice cream, and people-watch is this National Historic Landmark. You will have the ideal opportunity to see the lovely New York City tree lighting event if you travel around Christmas. Enjoy skating on the renowned ice rink located beneath the Prometheus monument.

24.Attend a performance at Radio City Music Hall.

The fantastic precision dancing show, The Rockettes, is located at Radio City, which is only across the street from the Rock. This location, also referred to as the "Showplace of the Nation," hosts a wide range of important events and concerts, including Cirque du Soleil and the NFL Draft. The 2017 RCMH entertainment lineup is impressive and features ballet, singing, edgy comedy, and their extraordinary Christmas extravaganza.

25. Shop for jewels in the Diamond District.

After Nazi Germany captured European diamond centers in Amsterdam and Antwerp, New York City's diamond district was essentially founded on 47th Street. The majority of the industry's Orthodox Jews emigrated to America and contributed to the development of the nation's most significant thoroughfare for the purchase, sale, and creation of magnificent wholesale or custom jewelry. There are countless diamond shops and a large number of amiable gemologists. Having conversations and haggling with them is a lot of fun. They are professionals, so take care not to try to trick them.

26.Dance in the Rainbow Room

This storied location near Rockefeller Center offers magnificent vistas of Manhattan along with delectable meals. This is the pinnacle of beautiful, traditional fine dining. Men must wear a coat and tie, and women should dress elegantly for the evening when visiting the Rainbow Room. A big-band ensemble will perform outstanding jazz or Count Basie-inspired music at Bar Sixty Five as you dance away the evening. You'll always remember that fantastic evening.

27. Take a tour of the New York Public Library.

The Library of Congress in Washington, D.C., is the largest library in the country; this one is ranked second. To maintain order and a collection of 53 million books, magazines, antiques, and digital materials, NYPL has a sizable annual budget of $245 million. Don't pass on this outstanding and big collection because there aren't many books you can't find. Never before has getting lost in the maze of bookshelves been so much fun. Imagine ordering everyone to be silent from a team of more than 3,000 people.

28.Visit the Chrysler Building

Since it was constructed in 1930, this skyscraper has become one of the most recognizable in the entire globe. The Chrysler is remains the tallest brick-faced structure in the world at 1,046 feet and is best recognized for its complex Art-Deco style roofing.

Visit the observation deck and take a tour of this magnificent structure with a guide.

29.Intrepid Sea, Air, and Space Museum

One of the few occasions when you'll visit Hell's Kitchen on the West Side is for this. The naval, air, and space endeavors of the United States are celebrated in this outstanding show on the Hudson River. Take a tour of the enormous aircraft carrier USS Intrepid and look inside the Enterprise and Concord spacecraft. Even better, you may virtually board the submarine USS Growler and marvel at the SR 71, the world's fastest spy plane.

30. Go on a Circle Line cruise.

No matter how much fun you've had, you're tired of walking, hiking, and dragging yourself through the New York traffic. The answer is to take a leisurely Circle Line trip across New York Harbor. Enjoy a sumptuous dinner and some robust potables while touring areas of New Jersey, Staten Island, Brooklyn, and Manhattan. If the weather is favorable, It is recommended taking the evening tour since it is incredible to see the New York skyline from the boat railing. However, reservations are essential.

Downtown

Greenwich Village, China Town, and Wall Street are all located in the neighborhood below 34th Street.

31.Visit the Empire State Building

The 1,454-foot-tall Empire State Building, which has 102 stories, has been a symbol of American culture since its 1931 debut. For good cause, it has subsequently been dubbed one of the Seven Wonders of the Modern World. The view from the observation deck of the Empire is much more wide than the view from the Chrysler Building. King Kong and Mighty Joe Young undoubtedly scaled the structure for that reason. However, they failed to pay for their tickets and were shot as a result. Avoid the same error by purchasing a ticket and using the elevator; you'll have a good time.

32. Attend Madison Square Garden to watch sports.

New Yorkers go to MSG to see significant athletic events. This storied location played host to some of the most memorable basketball championship games (Bulls vs. Knicks) and boxing contests (Ali vs. Frazier) in American sports history. The Garden also hosts rock concerts, Disney on Ice performances, hockey games, MMA wrestling matches, and circus performances. There is usually a significant event taking on at the Garden; check their website.

33.Eat at Eleven Madison Park.

The world's best restaurant of 2016 was Eleven Madison, a Michelin Three Star establishment, according to 1,000 food journalists, chefs, and gourmets who convened in Melbourne, Australia. They chose 50 of the world's best restaurants, with Eleven Madison at the top of the list.

The cuisine on the menu is of the highest caliber and is dubbed "contemporary French with a twist of New York." These are fixed-price meals that include nine courses of both shared and private food. The off-menu meal of Lavender and Honey Duck can also be to your liking. Make reservations and have a strong credit card with you. Life only comes around once, so live it up.

34.Visit Greenwich Village

The bohemian equivalent of San Francisco's Haight Ashbury is New York City's Greenwich Village. Artists, poets, writers, and pseudo-intellectuals live in this area. The Lower West Side neighborhood of The Village is home to some pretty intriguing coffee shops, trinket stores, sushi bars (organic of course), and edgy comedy clubs. Spend some time at the charming Washington Square Park and observe how the residents interact with nature (organic of course).

35. Explore Chinatown.

Booking a two-hour guided walking tour is the best way to truly understand China Town. This Lower East Side cultural and culinary hotspot took the place of the notorious Five Points area that was the subject of Martin Scorsese's epic film Gangs of New York. China Town, which is now more civilized, features amazing tea houses, open-air marketplaces, restaurants, and shops selling silk.

36.Visit the City Hall.

Even though City Hall is unbeatable, you should still go see this important National Landmark. The government building is the oldest continuously operating City Hall in the country and is situated in the heart of the lovely City Hall Park. Both the City Council Chambers and "Hizzoner the Mayor's" office are located there.

37. Give the Bull a kiss.

This massive bronze sculpture weighs 7,100 pounds and is 11 feet tall and 16 feet long. It is located at the Bowling Green Plaza at Broadway and Morris Street. It features an enormous charging bull, which has come to represent the nation's bold financial optimism and prosperity. If you rub and kiss the bull's nose, you will obtain wealth beyond your wildest expectations.

38.The New York Stock Exchange should be visited.

The NYSE is what Wall Street is all about, representing the very center of global capitalism. It is the biggest stock exchange in the world and is in charge of trading assets worth more than $175 billion every working day. The market capitalisation of companies listed on the NYSE is greater than $20 trillion. This is where the actual, significant money is made, in other words. Since you're already in the area, you might as well see how it's done to determine whether kissing the bull was successful.

39.Relax in Trinity Church.

For more than 300 years, this distinctive and stunning Episcopal church has played a significant role in New York's history. It is closely related to the Church of England, which bought the property in 1696. With all the financial wheeling and dealing going on around it, this place is actually a calm haven. During the terrorist attack on 9/11/2001, Trinity Church provided hundreds of people with a warm place to hide.

40. Visit Delmonico's for a beverage.

Go have a drink at Delmonico's Steak House if you want to see what true Wall Street moguls look like. This historic watering place for Wall Street traders has been located on the same triangle corner of Beaver and William Streets since 1837, only one block from the NYSE. The restaurant was the first in America to provide printed menus.

Acquire a drink at the bar because it's practically impossible to get a table during the workweek. Enjoy watching men try to keep their $40 martinis from getting on their $500 silk ties. You should arrive there before six if witnessing Wallstreat's big names is your goal. After then, everyone will have already left for the Hamptons.

41.In Battery Park, unwind.

On Manhattan's southern edge, below the financial sector, is another peaceful area called The Battery. It offers a stunning view of the Statue of Liberty, Staten Island, New Jersey, and New York Harbor. Visit the beautiful Eagle Statue, the East Coast Memorial, the Merchant Mariners' Memorial, and the Sphere of Hope Garden while you're there. The close-up view of the Manhattan skyline will also be enjoyable.

42.Lunch at Dead Rabbit Grocery & Grog.

The best bar in the world is located in New York City, which also has some of the best restaurants in the entire globe. Before seeing the Statue of Liberty and the 9/11 Memorial, stop by The Dead Rabbit, a trendy restaurant on the southern point of Manhattan.

It is known for offering outstanding hand-crafted cocktails and has an Irish theme. Spend time in the pub on the first floor or enjoy a drink in the elegant main parlor above. Take lots of photos and drink a "toddy for the body." The restaurant offers a wide variety of drinks and savory meals in sizable amounts

43. Visit the 9/11 Memorial to pay respects.

The city took more than ten years to complete and performed an outstanding job of rebuilding the site of the 9/11/2001 attacks, which claimed 2,977 lives. The Twin Towers' crash site has been restored, and the distinctive architecture of the stunning new structures nearby have moved and impressed many.

More than 11,000 objects, works of art, books, and documents related to the tragedy can be seen when you tour the museum. There are also over 40,000 print and digital images to look over. Each victim's name is carved in black marble on the South Pool. There isn't a dry eye in sight.

44.Visit the Statue of Liberty,

Not your grandfather's kind of vacation spot, this. The ferry voyage offers a breathtaking view of Manhattan's skyline and a close-up of Ellis Island, the former entry point for people from the old world to the United States. Lady Liberty, a magnificent copper monument standing 305 feet tall on her elaborate pedestal, is situated in Upper New York Bay.

As a gift from France, the statue was erected in 1886 to honor the young political and social experiment known as America. Although Gustave Eiffel—yes, that Eiffel—built it, Frederic Bartholdi designed it.

45. visit the Immigration Museum

Make sure to visit the Ellis Island immigration museum if you're searching for something to do while on vacation that will teach you a little bit of history or help you learn something. Millions of individuals traveled to Ellis Island on their way to the United States. You must go and visit this spot because of all the history associated with it. You will discover all of the individual tales of those who made the decision to immigrate to America in search of a fresh start. You might even be able to learn a little something about some of your own kin.

Take the same route that these immigrants did to enter the country for the first time when you are there. You may navigate every area, including baggage claim, the registry, and even the hearing rooms, exactly as they did. Some of these individuals even fled the nation under different names than when they arrived. You cannot discover this period of history in any other region of the nation, thus it is worthwhile to look through it.

You can visit the American Family History Center if a member of your family arrived in our country through this gateway. You can learn the history of some of your own ancestors in this section, which will provide some genealogical records on a computer.

46.Tour the Alice Austen House Museum & Garden

Located on Staten Island, the Alice Austen House Museum and Gardens brings to mind the reconstruction of the world of Alice Austen, an exceptional photographer. The beautiful Victorian style cottage offers stunning vistas over New York Harbor and features some impressive photographs, prints and glass negatives from her life's works illustrating what life was like in America at the end of the 19th century and the beginning of the 20th.

The Alice Austen house was purchased by the City in 1975 and brought it back to life during the mid-1980s. Taking inspiration from Austen's own photos, a team of gardeners worked tirelessly to recreate it in a truly authentic Victorian style. Mulberry bushes and flowering quince, along with an array of other shrubs and flowers were planted, offering a relaxing and genuine olde-worlde atmosphere. The collection of negatives and other artifacts on display here are owned by the Staten Island Historical Society, who runs the museum at the same time, allowing a glimpse into the life and work of this amazing woman.

47. Go to The American Craft Museum

Located on Fifth Avenue, the American Craft Museum is situated in the heart of the city's central business region. The museum sits opposite MoMA in a building that resembles an office. Inside, the museum is divided into several galleries of which are arranged in a strangely distinctive way, on a succession of verandas with bowed flights of stairs connecting each other to different floors. Much of the artifacts displayed are of modern design although many aren't in the typical abstract fashion contemporary art is recognized for. Some of the artworks are so crazy it can leave you quite amused, whereas others have a distinctive social message that tugs at the heart. The museum holds a multitude of temporary exhibitions that are changed regularly. The museum offers a fun and interesting time so make sure to devote around two hours to see everything.

48. visit Museum of Arts and Design

The Museum of Arts and Design is a great place to visit for a few hours if you enjoy learning about modern history's progress in art, craft and design. The museum holds an interesting collection of objects dedicated to this subject, as well as offering a range of educational programs for visitors of all ages.

49. visit American Folk Art Museum

Originally known as the Museum of Early American Folk Arts when it opened in 1961, the American Folk Art Museum is dedicated to the further understanding of the traditional arts and craftworks of the 18th and 19th centuries in America. There is a huge emphasis on the arts coming out of the northeast of the country. It has earned a strong international reputation for being a leading institution dedicated to this particular timeframe on American folk art. The museum is divided into various galleries, including sections devoted to folk art from other countries, as well as offering a range of educational programs to visitors.

The name of the museum was changed in 1966 in the expectation of gaining a strong reputation and dynamic growth. The American Folk Art Museum has offered temporary exhibitions showcasing the folk art from Norway, the United Kingdom and Latin America to name but a few. Other interesting artifacts on display include quilts, portraits, pottery, boxes, religious paintings and crucifixes, many of which you couldn't expect to see in other New York City museums. Expect to spend around two hours here.

50.Pass through American Museum of the Moving Image

The American Museum of the Moving Image is dedicated to illustrating the history and art of moving images, of which has become one of the most powerful creative and social impact in the last 100 years. The museum showcases some wonderful objects and is well known for housing the most significant collection of motion pictures and objects from television. The collection gracefully showcases how art and moving images are close.

Also on display are reflective film sequences, which are regularly supplemented by talks with the producers of the movies themselves, as well as media conferences with people from the actual industry. Students studying humanities, science and art from various grades come here regularly to take part in the different educational programs on offer.

When visiting the American Museum of the Moving Image, be sure to visit the Behind the Screen exhibition. Here, you will learn how moving images were produced, market and unveiled throughout history. The exhibition consists of over a thousand movie and television artifacts, media interactive experiences, audio and visual materials, along with presentations of specialized paraphernalia and procedures.

51. Tour American Numismatic Society

The American Numismatic Society is situated in the Audubon Terrace Cultural Complex and was established to be the foremost nation-wide organization in progressing the research and understanding of coins and medals, along with all other related items. The American Numismatic Society contains around 750,000 coins and other related items and enjoys an internationally renowned standard that is only rivaled by other collections in Europe. There are an amazing series of collections here, with many rare items on show. Some of the best collections are from ancient Greece, especially the Hellenistic section. The collections of Roman Republican items and the Islamic sections are well worth viewing. Be sure to pay attention to the Far Eastern displays (particularly the Chinese ones), the Latin American and the American items from both the colonial period as well as the Federal issues. There is a wonderful selection from private collections.

52. visit the Asian Society

The Asian Society is the best place to go to for understanding the long relationship between the American people and the cultures of Asia and the Pacific. In recent years, the relationship between Asia and America has strengthened and as such, there has been a need to provide a place to go to in order to understand Asia. The building itself has recently undergone a dramatic and extensive renovation in New York City, costing around $30 million. The galleries inside the museum are beautifully styled, and the general facilities and educational programs established have allowed it to gain a strong reputation as the one organization in America that concentrates on the connection of the arts, economics, political affairs and cultures throughout the Asia-Pacific region.

53. visit Bronx Museum of the Arts

The Bronx Museum of the Arts, which first opened to the public in 1971, features exhibitions and galleries that are both exciting and interesting for adults and kids. More than 800 works of art from every genre created in the 20th and 21st centuries are housed inside the museum.

The goal of the Bronx Museum of the Arts was to provide, primarily via the visual arts, a dynamic and engaging environment for the diverse ethnic groups residing in the Bronx. The enduring collections reflect the region's diverse ethnic communities, which include members of the African American, Latino, and Asian ethnicities.

54. Tour The Brooklyn Botanic Garden

An oasis in the center of the city is the Brooklyn Botanic Gardens. Being one of the largest cities on the planet, New York City has a reputation for being rather bustling and unclean. But if you want to escape the city's congestion and unwind in picturesque surroundings, head to the lovely Brooklyn Botanic Gardens. Every year, more than 750,000 visitors come to the Brooklyn Botanic Gardens to view more than 12,000 different types of flora from all over the world.

The renowned Steinhardt Conservatory's 52 acres contain the plants that are on display. There are multiple ponds teeming with different fish and turtles; the fountain in front of the Steinhardt Conservatory is stocked with enormous goldfish; and rabbits can be seen hopping in and out of the gardens; families can play a game to see how many of them they can spot while there.

The flora on exhibit has been brought in from all over the world, and the bulk of it is clearly labeled with both its scientific and common names. Since there is a lot of ground to cover, it is recommended to get a map at the entry and take your time exploring the many winding, obscure roads that lead to breathtakingly beautiful places.

The Brooklyn Botanical Gardens have a number of themed areas, including a Japanese Zen garden, a rose garden, a garden of native plants, and an exquisite rock garden. Head to the garden's seating area, which is lined with cherry trees, whenever you need a moment of relaxation or want to take in the scenery for a little longer. For individuals who want to learn more about the various ecosystems in the world, the conservatory is the perfect place. Here, you may see ecosystems from the tropics, the desert, and the sea.

The Brooklyn Botanical Gardens is the ideal tourist destination for families. You can spend anywhere from an hour to a whole day there, but because so much of the gardens are outdoors, you should dress appropriately for the season. Since educational outings to the Brooklyn Botanical Gardens are quite popular, you should be prepared to observe schoolchildren of all ages here.

55. Go to The Brooklyn Museum of Art

If you are interested in Ancient Egyptian art then the Brooklyn Museum of Art is the ideal place to visit. In addition to holding some of the best Egyptian artworks in the entire world, they also include fabulous collections of Classical, Mesopotamian, African, Pacific and American artworks from all periods. There are 28 rooms dedicated to art from various locations and periods for guests to be amazed at. Every first Saturday of the month, the Brooklyn Museum of Art holds a special program, the topic of which varies.

56. Visit the Central Park Zoo and Tisch Children's Zoo

If you're visiting New York with kids of any age, head to the Wildlife Centre at Central Park Zoo. From the tiny leafcutter ants to the captivating and majestic polar bears, students will encounter a wide variety of animals here from all over the world. Don't miss any of the fascinating exhibits at the Central Park Zoo. You can embark on a journey through the Tropic Zone, which features a rainforest environment and is home to birds and monkeys, then explore the Temperature Territory, where you can see monkeys swinging from tree branches and sea lions playing in the water. Finally, brave the Polar Circle and be mesmerized by the polar bears swimming through the Plexiglas enclosure, along with penguins and pygmy walrus

Visit the lovely Tisch Children's Zoo, which was designed for smaller children in mind, if your child is under six years old. Here, kids may get up close and personal with a variety of friendly and gentle creatures, including goats, pigs, lambs, turtles, frogs, cows, and more. The primary zoo admission tickets include admission.

You may buy food from machines, and the animals will happily eat right out of your hands, making it a delightful experience for the younger ones.

The American Zoo and Aquarium Association's Species Survival Program, which is committed to assisting a variety of species listed as endangered, has the Central Park Zoo actively involved in a number of initiatives. Tamarin monkeys, red pandas, and thick-billed parrots are just a few examples of these critters. In order to encourage people to learn more about the planet we live in, the people who live in it, and how we can help protect it, the Central Park Zoo also offers a number of seminars and events in addition to its well-known Wildlife Theatre. Outside the enclosures, feeding hours and animal-related talks are posted.

57. Visit The Children's Museum of the Art

The Children's Museum of the Arts is a must-see attraction for kids under ten. They can develop their artistic talent through a variety of forms of art thanks to the museum's entertaining and interesting exhibitions and programs. The museum has a strong emphasis on inclusion, creating a variety of agendas that especially incorporate kids with various special needs and their families into the essence of the museum itself.

It can be challenging to find the Children's Museum of the Arts because it is sandwiched between two business buildings close to Chinatown. The museum is frequently disregarded because it doesn't appear to have any other cultural attractions on the street. Watch out for the recognizable zebra monument and the brightly colored windows.

There are several different areas in the museum. The Artist's Studio resembles a genuine operating studio in appearance. Children can do a variety of art projects using a variety of artistic materials, and occasionally some local artists will come and provide a hand. The Actor's Studio offers a variety of costumes and tales to act out, which encourages kids' interest in drama and the theater. Any child who needs aid with their fine motor skills can benefit from playing in the Ball Pond. This area is covered in the brightly colored physio balls, making it a fantastic place to take children for their first visit to the museum. You can find a variety of fantastic works of art that have been carved into puzzle pieces in the Magnetic Masterpieces area. While learning about the original artist, their time and place of residence, and how they affected the history of art, children will develop their motor skills.The Children's Museum of the Arts is a must-see attraction for kids under ten. They can develop their artistic talent through a variety of forms of art thanks to the museum's entertaining and interesting exhibitions and programs. The museum has a strong emphasis on inclusion, creating a variety of agendas that especially incorporate kids with various special needs and their families into the essence of the museum itself.

It can be challenging to find the Children's Museum of the Arts because it is sandwiched between two business buildings close to Chinatown. The museum is frequently disregarded because it doesn't appear to have any other cultural attractions on the street. Watch out for the recognizable zebra monument and the brightly colored windows.

There are several different areas in the museum. The Artist's Studio resembles a genuine operating studio in appearance. Children can do a variety of art projects using a variety of artistic materials, and occasionally some local artists will come and provide a hand. The Actor's Studio offers a variety of costumes and tales to act out, which encourages kids' interest in drama and the theater. Any child who needs aid with their fine motor skills can benefit from playing in the Ball Pond. This area is covered in the brightly colored physio balls, making it a fantastic place to take children for their first visit to the museum. You can find a variety of fantastic works of art that have been carved into puzzle pieces in the Magnetic Masterpieces area. While learning about the original artist, their time and place of residence, and how they affected the history of art, children will develop their motor skills.

58.Shop at Bergdorf Goodman

Given that some of the biggest retailers in the world are located here, New York City is a veritable destination for shoppers. Although there are several shopping areas in New York City, Fifth Avenue from 57th Street to the upper 40s is where Manhattan's retail is at its most vibrant. Some of the most well-known flagship stores welcome customers with high-end goods here.

The oldest department stores in the US, including Henri Bendel, Bergdorf Goodman, and Saks Fifth Avenue, are also located on Fifth Avenue. Although the majority of tourists don't really have the money to make significant purchases in these shops, their distinctive and opulent displays are nevertheless a good enough reason to go there.

Bergdorf Goodman is the most magnificent department store. In actuality, this upscale store has two locations that are one across from the other. The department store was established in 1899 by Herman Bergdorf, a French immigrant. It started out as a tailor shop close to Union Square. The store's name was changed to Bergdorf Goodman in 1901 after one of Bergdorf's apprentices, Edwin Goodman, purchased a portion of the company two years later.

The store was relocated to 32nd Street five years later, not too far from where it is now. Bergdorf had no interest in growing its clientele, so Goodman acquired his share of the store and helped the business become even more prosperous.

On the site of Cornelius Vanderbilt the II's mansion, at Fifth Avenue and 58th Street, Goodman constructed a Beaux-Arts structure in 1928. This building is also where the store is now.

Under the direction of Andrew Goodman, son of Edwin Goodman, the upscale department store was sold to another American merchant in 1972. The upscale department store has since undergone numerous expansions, and in 1990, the men's store was moved directly across the street to make place for new women's boutiques.

Eight levels make up the structure today, and some of the establishments feature dressing rooms with stunning views of Central Park.

59. Visit the Coney Island

Coney Island is a popular destination for New Yorkers who wish to get away from the city's crowded, noisy streets. The area, which is technically a peninsula and is a residential neighborhood in Brooklyn, is well known for its amusement parks.

The first structures on Coney Island were constructed in the 1840s, and shortly after, the region developed into a well-liked vacation destination with amusement parks and beachside dining. Coney Island was, in reality, the biggest amusement park in the country. The neighborhood lost its appeal after World War II, and the majority of the theme parks were shut down. Coney Island, however, has recently come back into fashion and is once more New York's playground.

There are around 50 different rides and attractions on Coney Island, but the Wonder Wheel, a huge Ferris wheel with stunning views of Manhattan from the top, and the Cyclone, a roller coaster inaugurated in 1927, are the most well-known ones.

The most popular amusement park is Luna Park, which is located on Surf Avenue. The first one debuted in 1903 and shuttered more than 40 years later. A second theme park using the same name was opened in 2010, restoring Coney Island to its former splendor. Luna Park has 19 rides, ranging from the thrilling Thunderbolt to the family-friendly Tea Party, in addition to the iconic Cyclone roller coaster.

Hundreds more rides are available for visitors to enjoy outside of Luna Park at places like Deno's Wonder Wheel Amusement Park, Eldorado Arcade, Kiddie Park, and numerous other amusement parks.

A long, wide sandy beach that extends for more than two miles from West 37th Street begins at Coney Island. Despite the fact that several areas of the beach also offer many rides, this is Coney Island's second most visited attraction after the amusement parks.

60. Visit Grant's Tomb

Ulysses S. Grant was inaugurated into office as president for two terms and was one of the great generals to fight in the American

Civil War. Grant's Tomb is the eternal resting place of both him and his wife, sleeping for all eternity in two stunning sarcophagi that were created with Napoleon's tomb in Les Invalides, Paris, in mind. The mausoleum is fashioned from white granite and has stunning views over the Hudson River. Construction of the mausoleum and Riverside Park was finished in 1897, and inside visitors can view an amazing array of memorabilia and artifacts from the Civil War period. Entrance is free to everyone and is open every day of the week.

Chapter 5:

Shopping in New York

Most tourists to New York expect—no, they hope—for some real shopping therapy. Because you will have a lot of options, bring your plastic. Every significant chain retailer you can imagine is present in New York, and then some. Additionally, you can browse thousands of independent niche stores. It's a serious shopping experience, so make a strategy if you want to make the most of it. Here is a list of shrewd shopping advice and locations in New York where you may shop 'til you drop. Enjoy!

Shopping for deals in New York

In New York, not everything is pricey. There are deals to be found if you know where to search in this enormous city's many different stores. Designer clothing, jewelry, literature, and music, among many other products, are all available at steep prices. East Village's St. Marks Place. With its assortment of unique individual stores, the neighborhood has been compared to London's Camden Town. There is a fantastic street market there.

If you like designer clothing, stop by **Century 21 in Brooklyn** to get up to 75% off regular prices. However, bargain hunting can be a bit of an extreme sport around here because some shoppers would do anything to get their hands on a good deal. Forget about acting ladylike and just enter the store to nab those deals. You want to, you know it!

Gabay's Outlet on the Lower East Side is a great spot to find designer goods for up to 80% off the retail price. You may purchase everything from any designer you can imagine right here. All the top designers, like Gucci, Ralph Lauren, Chloe, and Chanel, can be found here, whether you're shopping for swimwear, accessories, styles, lingerie, casual clothing, or evening attire. The savings grow as the list is expanded.

The sample sales, which take place all year long, are still another thing to keep an eye out for. In essence, this is a clearance sale of designer clothing from the previous season, and you can find items for about 10% of the original cost. Be sure it's what you actually want before giving over the cash because it's typically cash only and there are no refunds. Avoiding the midday crowds is a smart idea as well because most of the items are laid out in boxes that you must search through. For that, you'll need some room to move.

Sample Sale Tips

- You should check the website to see what forms of payment are allowed, as many only accept cash or credit cards.
- Since many sales will ask you to check your baggage, only bring the bare minimum of "things" (purses, coats, etc.).
- Don't rely on changing rooms. They are present at some sales but not others, and when they are, there may be very long lineups. Learn the sizes for each brand.
- For sales where you are not required to check your luggage, bring a sizable empty bag. particularly for the sale of Manolo Blahnik shoes. After that, take five or more pairs at a time and try them on in the middle of the room. You will miss out while others are grabbing your preferred pairs of shoes if you choose to try on a pair at a time.
- Lacking money yet a nasty shopping habit? Check out Neiman Marcus, Bergdorf Goodman, and Barneys before you travel to discover what's popular right now. Purchase a few extra pairs of shoes, then sell them on eBay. You'll

most likely get your money's worth back plus your own sneakers for free.

- Some sales (again, like Manolo) demand that the checkout clerks use a marker to label your shoes' insoles. Ask the check-out girls VERY politely to lessen the amount of magic marker lines they draw through the Manolo tag. When you reach home, use a cotton swab and nail paint remover to gently and delicately rub the lines away. Voila! $100 for brand-new shoes!

Aside from its high-end fashion, New York is renowned for its affordable electronics. Spend less money by purchasing a laptop, tablet, smartphone, or camera. Greatest Buy is arguably the best place to buy gadgets, and there are several locations in New York, including ones on Fifth Avenue, Broadway, and Times Square.

It is recommended to go and find some of the discount stores if you are on a tight budget but still want to be able to get some items that are authentically from the city. They can be challenging at times, but doing some research and knowing where the restrooms are before you leave can help. Without having to spend a lot of money, you will be able to leave the city with a lot of wonderful presents for your friends, family, and yourself.

retail establishments

If you enjoy shopping in one place, you might want to visit some of New York's department stores. There are some well-known brands, and many shoppers will pay anything to leave the store with a Macy's or Bloomingdale's bag. Ladies might be interested in exploring Saks on Fifth Avenue's first floor marble salon, which has an enormous assortment of cosmetics and colognes. All of your potential shopping needs are covered on the 10 floors, and since St. Patrick's Cathedral is nearby, you can visit it once you've finished shopping.

You may browse the merchandise on 10 floors at **Macy's**, which has been labeled "the world's largest store," and if it all seems a little overwhelming, you can schedule a personal shopper appointment. They will search for what you need and deliver it to you for inspection as you unwind. The Cellar in the basement has a superb assortment of food and kitchen supplies if you enjoy fine dining and cooking.

Another "must-visit" store with a wide selection of goods for the entire family is B**loomingdale's.** Don't expect to discover haute couture there because of their preference for more casual attire. You will undoubtedly leave this venerable business with something useful, though.

Depending on where you live, you may have heard of one of these establishments or maybe visited one at some point.

However, nothing beats visiting the original and best of them and taking advantage of what they have to offer. Make sure to stop by these shops. You will be able to enjoy the entire experience of shopping in these places even if you decide not to buy anything or discover that it is too pricey.

Fifth Street

Fifth Avenue has always been associated with wealth and luxury, and the shopping experiences there undoubtedly uphold this reputation that was established during the time of The Great Gatsby. Check out the chic Italian restaurant and cocktail bar in the opulent Armani store. Finally, there is the renowned Tiffany's jewelry store, which contrasts most favorably with the more extravagant shops along Fifth Avenue.

Along Fifth Avenue, other well-known businesses include FAO Schwarz, a toy store, the Apple store, Bergdorf Goodman, Trump Tower, and the Rockefeller Center. There is a lot to look at even if you don't discover anything to purchase.

When you've finished shopping, return to the Plaza Hotel for afternoon tea in the renowned and iconic Palm Court. People-watching is possible there beneath the stunning stained-glass roof.

If they don't have much money to spend when visiting New York, some tourists choose to spend a little time here and buy a few nice things to celebrate before spending the rest of their trip in the outlet malls. This enables them to be a little extravagant, but by shopping at places with greater discounts, they will be able to save money on the rest of their gifts.

You can always reserve a shopping trip if the magnitude of New York's shopping experience overwhelms you. Prices for tours typically start at roughly $45 per person, but you'll receive discount vouchers that might save you a lot more than that. It's merely one more strategy to maximize your time in New York.

Ensure that you are establishing a plan before you go shopping. The trips mentioned above can be a terrific method to complete the process, but you must have some sort of plan in place. This makes it possible for you to plan your spending and keep within your means while still having a memorable experience.

Conclusion

It's one thing to read about a place, but it's another to experience it first-hand. New York City is a diverse oasis of beauty and culture. It's the center of a magnificent universe that has a little something for everyone. People of all ages come to New York City with wonderment and leave with new-found inspiration.

There is truly something for everyone in New York City. There are zoos, world-famous art museums, exquisite restaurants, parks, shopping, historic landmarks and so many other amazing places to see and fantastic things to do. We have curated some of the best things to do in New York City but by no means is it all-inclusive.

Printed in Great Britain
by Amazon

25977042R00066